9/16

INSIDE THE
HUMAN BODY

NERVOUS SYSTEM

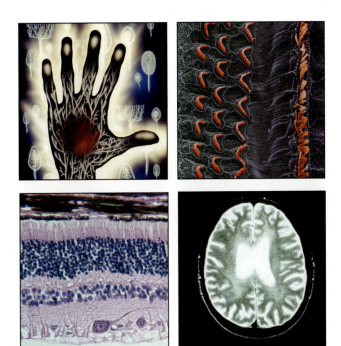

by Steve Parker

New
Forest
Press

How to use this book

This book is your guide to yourself—an atlas of the human body. Follow the main text for an informative overview of a particular area of the body or use the boxes to jump to a specific area of interest. Finally, try some of the suggested activities and experiments to discover more about yourself!

Body Locator

Highlighted areas on the body locator help you learn your body's geography by indicating the area of the body organs or systems discussed on those pages.

Instant Info

Get instant, snappy facts that summarize the topic in just a few sentences. Discover how fast nerve signals travel, how many smells we can detect, and much more.

Health Watch

Read about illness and disease related to the relevant area of the body. For example, learn what happens if the brain suffers a heavy blow and how we can protect ourselves.

INSTANT FACTS

Short-term memories last a few seconds or minutes. Like a little-used phone number, such brief information is stored only as long as we need it.

Medium-term memories, such as what we ate recently, often last a few hours, or—at most—days.

Long-term memories last many years, even a lifetime.

Our powers of recall for a memory depend on its importance, its related sensory input, and how regularly our minds refresh it by thinking about, or revisiting, it.

HEALTH WATCH

We normally forget things. Our busy brains cannot always cope with the thousands of thoughts and distractions that occur every day. Very often, too much to do in too short a time leads to mental stress and forgetfulness.

BRAIN *LEARNING AND MEMORY*

When someone asks you for your name, home address, and phone number, you probably respond instantly. Remembering something like the number of windows in your home might take longer.

Finding Memories
We instantly remember vital information. But your brain provides an answer to the window question another way. Unless you expected that particular question, your "mind's eye" would probably go from room to room in your house, counting each window. This process not only illustrates our memory for names, faces, and facts, but also shows how our brain perceives scenes, smells, sounds, and countless other recollections.

Take a card, any card . . . . Your mind needs exercise, too. Mental exercises involving recall and retention, such as remembering which cards have been played and by whom, improve your memory by making it work more accurately and faster.

14

Try It Yourself

Try these suggested activities to learn more. No special equipment is required—just your own body!

**Metric Conversion Table
on page 31**

In Focus

View stunning macroimagery and other images of an anatomically correct digital model of body parts.

IN FOCUS
Clever Brain

The brain's temporoparietal region discriminates between true and false memories. Brain activity shows up as a red spot on this PET scan, indicating that the person recognized a familiar word.

In this scan, neurons fail to activate in response to an unfamiliar word—indicating no prior pathway, or memory.

HIPPOCAMPUS

The cortex temporarily stores short-term memories. Unless important or remembered several times, these memories soon disappear—just like erasing a text message from a cell phone. Long-term memories encoded and stored in the hippocampus may last a lifetime.

cortex

hippocampus

15

Our memory for faces is especially amazing. Some people can distinguish more than one hundred different faces from photographs after seeing each for only two seconds.

Disk Drive

Researchers cannot identify exactly where our brain stores such information. No single brain location does everything. Instead, many brain areas work together to learn, encode memories, and produce recall. These areas and structures include the outer layer of the cortex as well as the thalamus, amygdala, and hippocampus deep within the center of the brain. Memories most likely form as a particular set of connections between billions of neurons. Learning involves building a new brain pathway.

Learning More

Research on the human brain has brought an explosion of excitement and promise to our understanding of ourselves—how we think, how we learn, how the brain regulates activities and reacts to stimulation, and how we are the same and different, depending upon many, many aspects of the brain itself. There is still so much to learn and understand about our brains.

TRY IT YOURSELF

Improve your memory with a mnemonic, or memory trick. Make someone's name pop into your mind as soon as you see him or her by using the first letter of that name to form an association, or memory pathway. You might use "Einstein" for "Edward" (right), because he thinks deeply about things.

Diagrams

Watch for in-depth scientific diagrams and explanations that focus on the details of a body part.

CONTENTS

Introduction

How many thoughts have you had today? How often have you used your memory since you woke up? Even if you think hard, it's impossible to remember every detail. Thinking and remembering play important roles in our everyday lives, usually without us noticing.

The Puzzle of the Brain

Thoughts, memories, and automatic reactions occur within the brain millions of times each second. Determining how the brain works poses one of the greatest challenges facing scientists. Every year, we learn more about the dozens of different brain areas and how they send and receive nerve signals, or impulses. These nerve signals let us think, learn, remember, decide, act, move, and experience feelings and emotions. But the brain is so complicated that the more we know about it, the more we realize we must study it even further.

A Living "Internet"

Part of the challenge of understanding the brain is that it does not work alone. The brain and nerves form a living "Internet" called the nervous system: an amazing network of branching, wirelike nerves that links the brain to all parts of the body and communicates huge amounts of information at incredible speed.

Sensing the Surroundings

Like a supercomputer, the brain needs input—information coming into it. This information comes from the body's five senses: sight, hearing, smell, taste, and touch. But just like the nervous system, the sensory system is much more complex than it seems.

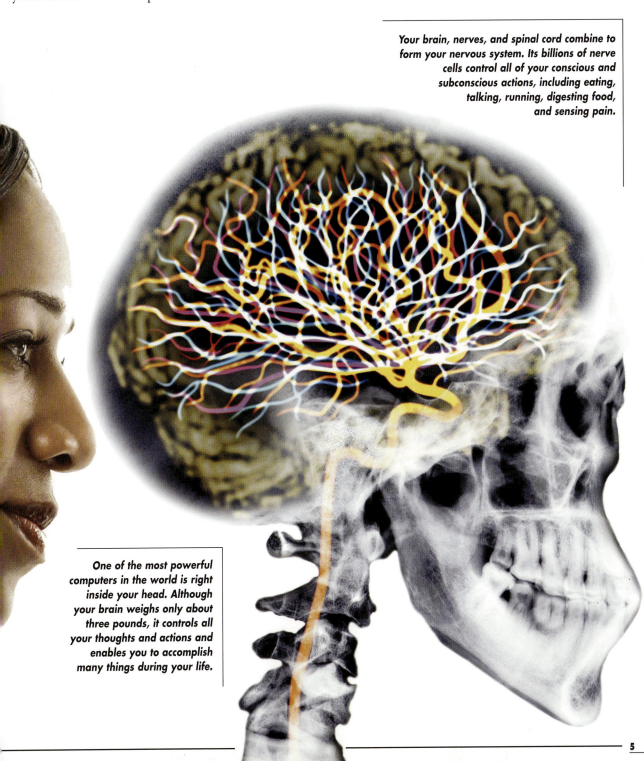

Your brain, nerves, and spinal cord combine to form your nervous system. Its billions of nerve cells control all of your conscious and subconscious actions, including eating, talking, running, digesting food, and sensing pain.

One of the most powerful computers in the world is right inside your head. Although your brain weighs only about three pounds, it controls all your thoughts and actions and enables you to accomplish many things during your life.

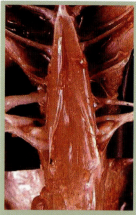
NERVES *THE NERVOUS SYSTEM*

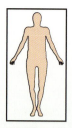

We call people who seem jumpy, slightly worried, and tense "nervous." But you could also say that everyone is nervous, all the time. In fact, our nerves never rest. They carry enormous amounts of information in the form of tiny electrical impulses, or nerve signals.

If all your nerves were joined end to end, they would stretch about sixty-two miles.

The sciatic nerves, your longest and thickest nerves, begin in the spinal cord and run down your leg from hip to heel.

A giraffe's longest nerve cell runs fifteen feet from its neck to its front toe.

A plexus is an area where several nerves meet, regroup, and branch out in a new neural network.

Central Nervous System

The brain and spinal cord form the central nervous system. The spinal cord connects to the base of the brain and runs down through the backbones, or vertebrae. Together, they work much like a computer's hard drive that controls many devices and machines attached to it. But a living control system requires not only a method of input and response but also another monitoring system that works behind the scenes to keep everything running smoothly.

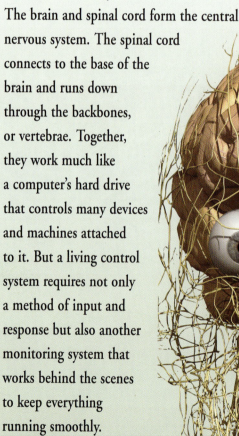

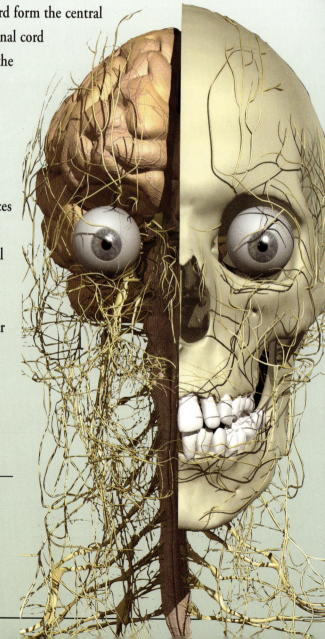

An intricate network of small nerves links the brain to the muscles and skin of the head and face. Such complicated "wiring" provides these highly sensitive areas with precise muscle control.

👁 **HEALTH WATCH**

A diet lacking certain vitamins and minerals can interfere with proper nervous function. Nerves need a regular supply of vitamins B_1, B_6, B_{12}, and E and the minerals calcium, sodium, potassium, and magnesium.

Support Systems

The peripheral nervous system, a network of nerves that branch from the brain and spinal cord out to various parts of the head and body, form a second component of the nervous system. The autonomic nerve system consists of areas inside the brain and spinal cord, nerves that run down both sides of the spinal cord, and nerves that reach into internal organs, such as the lungs, stomach, and heart. This portion of the nervous system controls processes that happen automatically without us thinking about them, including digesting food and regulating the heartbeat.

Every second, the brain receives huge amounts of information from the senses and sends out millions of signals to control the body's hundreds of muscles. That is why we must concentrate hard when learning a new activity, such as jet skiing or other sports. Our brains soon adapt, and many movements become second nature.

🦅 TRY IT YOURSELF

If your foot ever "fell asleep" while you sat in an awkward position, you probably felt the tingling sensation of "pins and needles" when you started moving again. This feeling warns that a nerve was squashed or that blood vessels supplying it were squeezed. End this feeling by moving, stretching, or rubbing until it feels better.

IN FOCUS
Head and Face

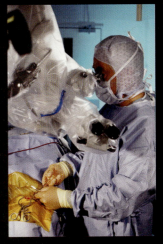

The brain, spinal cord, and delicate nerve tissues are easily harmed. Neurosurgeons specialize in operations on the brain and nerves. They sometimes work on a single nerve fiber that is finer than a human hair.

🦅 TWO OUT OF THREE

The central nervous system functions as the brain's main control center. The peripheral nervous system carries nerve impulses between the central nervous system and other body areas.

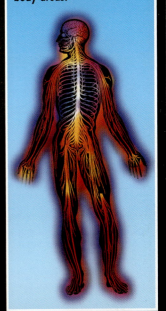

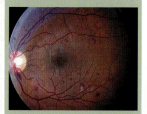

A single nerve signal lasts for 1/700 of a second.

Most nerve fibers can carry up to three hundred nerve signals per second.

The fastest nerve signals travel at about 265 miles per hour and travel from toe to brain in less than 1/100 of a second.

The slowest nerve signals travel at slightly more than two miles per hour.

NERVES GOT NERVES?

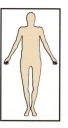

Our bodies automatically repair or replace some tissues and cells as they gradually wear away. The skin renews itself every month. You grow a new stomach lining every three days. Nerves are different and so complicated that they rarely get repaired or renewed.

Nerve Cells

Every nerve contains bundles of threadlike fibers of microscopic nerve cells, or neurons. The entire nervous system contains billions of neurons—tens of billions in the brain alone. Each neuron carries a tiny electrical signal.

HEALTH WATCH

Once a nerve is damaged or injured, it may take months or years to heal—if it does at all. When a nerve is unable to carry signals that make a muscle move, paralysis results. An inability of nerves to carry signals from the skin to the brain causes loss of feeling or numbness. Proper safety gear, such as helmets; wrist guards; shoulder, elbow, and knee pads; and goggles, provide personal protection from injury during risky activities or extreme sports.

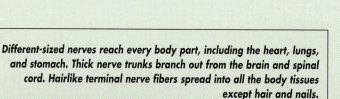

Different-sized nerves reach every body part, including the heart, lungs, and stomach. Thick nerve trunks branch out from the brain and spinal cord. Hairlike terminal nerve fibers spread into all the body tissues except hair and nails.

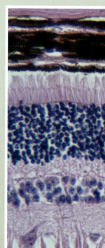

Coming and Going

A single neuron runs the entire length of a nerve and acts independently. The electrical signal from one nerve cell creates little effect. But when linked together with many other neurons, it forms an amazing network. Each nerve cell receives signals from thousands of other cells and in turn communicates those signals to thousands of other nerve cells. Nerve impulses travel along countless different pathways. And every day, as our thoughts and memories change, those nerve pathways also change.

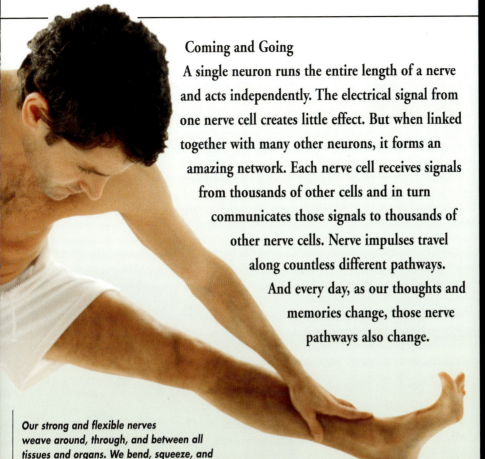

Our strong and flexible nerves weave around, through, and between all tissues and organs. We bend, squeeze, and squash various nerves with every movement.

Human nerve fibers are less than $1/1000$ of 0.04 of an inch wide. A squid's nerve cells are thicker than human hairs. The study of squid nerves added greatly to our knowledge of the nervous system.

Dendrites, short weblike projections, spike out from a nerve cell to receive signals and carry them to the cell's main body. A neuron's longer fiber, or axon, passes the signals along to other nerve cells at billions of synapses.

Slight gaps called synapses separate nerve fiber endings from each other. Electrical nerve signals in the form of natural body chemicals called neurotransmitters "jump" across the synapses.

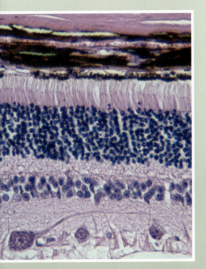

TRY IT YOURSELF

When you injure a toe or finger, you probably feel the touch on it a split second before the pain begins. Nerve signals from pressure receptors in the skin usually travel a fraction of a second faster than pain signals.

NERVE FASCICLES

Like phone cables, nerves consist of bunches of separate "wires" strung into one line. Connective tissue containing minute blood vessels and fat cells covers each individual nerve fiber, nerve bundle (fascicle), and group of fascicles. A nerve's outermost covering is called the epineurium.

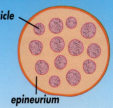

nerve fascicle

epineurium

The brain looks like a lump of pink-gray jelly. Despite its bland appearance, the brain is the site of all our mental processes, such as thinking, remembering, feeling sensations, and controlling our muscles. Surprisingly, the brain has no senses or muscles of its own and cannot feel pain.

Deep Within

While an image of the outer, wrinkled cerebrum comes to mind when someone mentions the human brain, one of its most important areas—the brain stem—lies deep within, between the cerebrum and the spinal cord. The brain stem controls automatic body processes. These include monitoring the heartbeat, digesting food, regulating breathing, and maintaining a constant body temperature.

The average adult human brain weighs about three pounds.

It contains tens of billions of nerve cells.

There is no link between brain size and intelligence.

The female brain is slightly larger in proportion to body size than that of a male.

A newborn's brain is about one-third its adult size. Before birth, a fetus grows 250,000 neurons per minute.

👁 HEALTH WATCH

Most people get occasional headaches. Someone who suffers a severe headache together with a stiff neck, aversion to bright lights, and perhaps a skin rash, may have a serious brain inflammation: meningitis. It occurs when the meninges—the coverings around the brain—swell because of a viral or bacterial infection. Meningitis needs urgent medical attention and care.

🦴 BRAIN REGIONS

A computer-generated image reveals the major brain regions. The cerebrum controls conscious ideas, thoughts, and actions. The cerebellum monitors our coordination by regulating muscle movement.

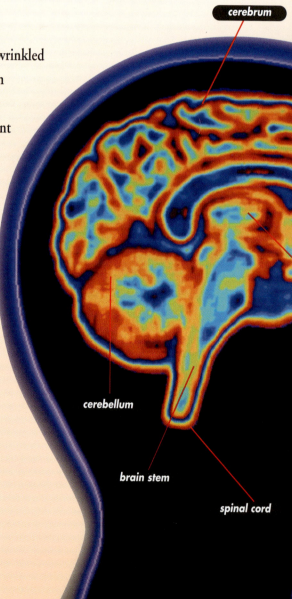

cerebrum

cerebellum

brain stem

spinal cord

Making Movements

A rounded, wrinkled area at the lower back of the brain, called the cerebellum, regulates muscle response. The cerebellum uses nerve signals from the cerebrum to control which muscles should tighten, by how much, and for how long. This information coordinates muscles to work as teams, making our movements smooth and precise.

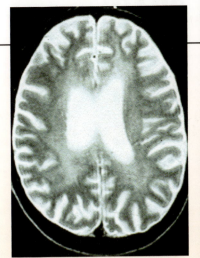

MRI (Magnetic Resonance Imaging) scans (above) show details of the brain's inner structure, including its many blood vessels. MRI scans help locate problems, such as lack of blood flow to part of the brain, that can cause the internal brain injury known as a stroke.

IN FOCUS
In and Around the Brain

A system of flattened hollow chambers called cerebral ventricles in the middle of the brain contain cerebrospinal fluid—the same liquid that bathes and cushions the brain and spinal cord.

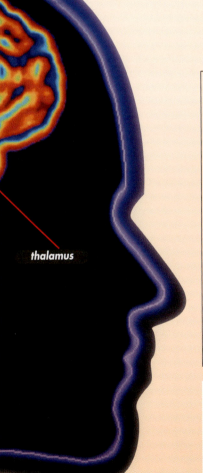

thalamus

Sensor pads attached to the skin of the head detect the millions of tiny electrical pulses that flash around the brain every second. A paper printout called an electro-encephalogram (EEG) records the pulses as squiggly lines. They show how the brain works and reveal disorders such as epilepsy.

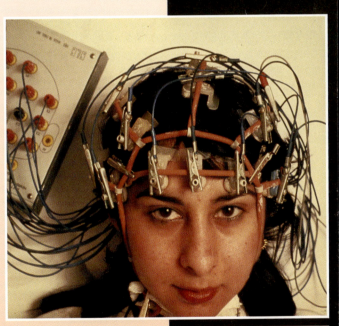

🖐 TRY IT YOURSELF

Gently tap the top of your head. It makes a dull thud. A thin layer of liquid called cerebrospinal fluid circulates around your brain underneath your skull. As you twist or move your head rapidly, or if something hits your head, the cerebrospinal fluid provides a moving cushion to protect from damage.

BRAIN MISSION CONTROL

Like NASA's (the National Aeronautics Space Administration's) control room in Houston, Texas, your brain functions as a living mission control center. It processes incoming and outgoing data; directs thoughts, actions, and movements; and monitors fuel consumption and other vital operations.

If spread out flat, the outer layer, or cortex, of the brain would cover the area of a standard pillowcase.

The cortex contains about twenty billion neurons.

Each neuron communicates with up to a quarter of a million other neurons.

Neurons give the cortex a grayish color, which is why the brain is sometimes called "gray matter."

Centers for Control

The cerebrum makes up more than three-quarters of your brain. Different areas of its highly organized outer layer, the cerebral cortex, specialize in controlling and monitoring sensory information, directing muscular response, and performing various mental tasks, such as creating memories, linking ideas (thinking), and developing your sense of "self"—the individual personality that makes you you.

👁 **HEALTH WATCH**

Asthma is an allergic condition that causes difficult and wheezy breathing. Dust, chemicals, or plant pollens floating in the air can bring on an allergic reaction, or asthma attack. Muscles in the airway walls tighten, and the linings of the airway and lungs produce more mucus, which clogs the system.

The brain's two sides look similar, but in most people, they play slightly different roles. The left brain usually processes analytical thoughts, helps you reason, and deals with numbers and facts. The right brain is often the center of creative thinking and artistic skills and helps you appreciate shapes, colors, and music.

A very deep groove runs along the middle of the brain from front to back and divides it into two cerebral hemispheres. Other deep grooves divide each hemisphere into five main sections, called lobes.

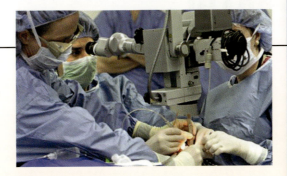

The brain cannot feel a scalpel or laser beam cut through its tissues. But the sensitive meninges—the three layers of protective covering that surround the brain—respond quickly to pain.

Centers for Senses

Specialized areas in the cerebral cortex respond to a different series of nerve impulses from sense receptors throughout the body. The brain's center for sight, located in the lower rear cortex, processes information about visual scenes. Hearing is processed in the auditory centers of the cortex on the sides of the brain. Touch receptors form a strip that arches over the top of the brain from side to side.

The upper front of each cerebral hemisphere is known as the frontal lobe. The frontal cortex covering it is important in what we call "personality" and in the awareness of the body's position in its surroundings. It keeps us from bumping into things!

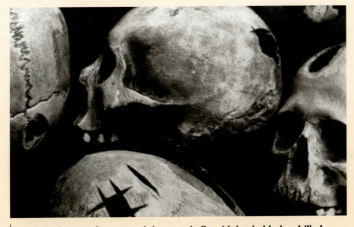

Archaeologists often unearth human skulls with healed holes drilled through them. Many ancient cultures used a procedure called trepanation, perhaps in an attempt to cure terrible headaches or as part of a ceremonial ritual. Trepanation, the earliest known form of surgery, began in the Stone Age. It is not medically practiced now.

Areas in the cerebral cortex control different senses, such as touch (pale blue-gray), speech (blue), hearing (red), and vision (dark yellow). The premotor cortex (light yellow) senses limb position. The motor cortex (orange) controls the muscles.

🖐 TRY IT YOURSELF

Can you write your name with your "other" hand? Try it. Your first few attempts will probably be terrible. Do this forty or fifty times, with short rests in between. Compare the last signature with the first. Your brain's motor center learned to make a new pattern of movements by using new nerve pathways.

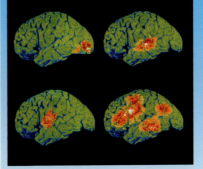

🔬 BUSY BRAIN

PET (positron emission tomography) scans show the brain's energy use and which regions are busiest. This series of PET images shows the left side of the brain in a person who is staring (upper left), listening (upper right), speaking (lower left), and thinking about talking and moving (lower right).

Short-term memories
last a few seconds or
minutes. Like a little-
used phone number,
such brief information
is stored only as long
as we need it.

Medium-term
memories, such as
what we ate recently,
often last a few hours,
or — at most — days.

Long-term memories
last many years, even
a lifetime.

Our powers of recall
for a memory depend
on its importance, its
related sensory input,
and how regularly our
minds refresh it by
thinking about, or
revisiting, it.

HEALTH WATCH

We normally forget things.
Our busy brains cannot
always cope with the
thousands of thoughts
and distractions that occur
every day. Very often, too
much to do in too short
a time leads to mental
stress and forgetfulness.

BRAIN *LEARNING AND MEMORY*

When someone asks you for your name, home address, and phone number, you probably respond instantly. Remembering something like the number of windows in your home might take longer.

Finding Memories

We instantly remember vital information. But your brain provides an answer to the window question another way. Unless you expected that particular question, your "mind's eye" would probably go from room to room in your house, counting each window. This process not only illustrates our memory for names, faces, and facts, but also shows how our brain perceives scenes, smells, sounds, and countless other recollections.

Take a card,
any card . . . .
Your mind needs
exercise, too. Mental
exercises involving
recall and retention,
such as remembering
which cards have
been played and by
whom, improve your
memory by making it
work more accurately
and faster.

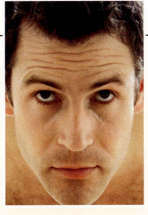

Our memory for faces is especially amazing. Some people can distinguish more than one hundred different faces from photographs after seeing each for only two seconds.

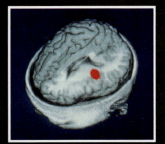

The brain's temporoparietal region discriminates between true and false memories. Brain activity shows up as a red spot on this PET scan, indicating that the person recognized a familiar word.

No Disk Drive

Researchers cannot identify exactly where our brain stores such information. No single brain location does everything. Instead, many brain areas work together to learn, encode memories, and produce recall. These areas and structures include the outer layer of the cortex as well as the thalamus, amygdala, and hippocampus deep within the center of the brain. Memories most likely form as a particular set of connections between billions of neurons. Learning involves building a new brain pathway.

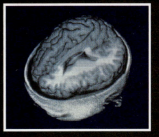

In this scan, neurons fail to activate in response to an unfamiliar word—indicating no prior pathway, or memory.

Learning More

Research on the human brain has brought an explosion of excitement and promise to our understanding of ourselves—how we think, how we learn, how the brain regulates activities and reacts to stimulation, and how we are the same and different, depending upon many, many aspects of the brain itself. There is still so much to learn and understand about our brains.

HIPPOCAMPUS

The cortex temporarily stores short-term memories. Unless important or remembered several times, these memories soon disappear—just like erasing a text message from a cell phone. Long-term memories encoded and stored in the hippocampus may last a lifetime.

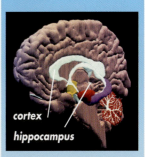

cortex

hippocampus

 TRY IT YOURSELF

Improve your memory with a mnemonic, or memory trick. Make someone's name pop into your mind as soon as you see him or her by using the first letter of that name to form an association, or memory pathway. You might use "Einstein" for "Edward" (right), because he thinks deeply about things.

BRAIN *Wide Awake, Fast Asleep*

After an exciting day of looking, learning, talking, and listening, you may feel wide awake. But five minutes after going to bed, you fall fast asleep. Your brain is far from switched off— it gets busy tending to many chores as you rest.

A newborn baby sleeps about twenty hours a day, every day.

Most ten-year-olds need about ten hours of sleep nightly.

Adults usually need seven to eight hours of sleep each night.

Some people function better with more than eight hours of sleep, while others feel good with fewer than six.

A sleep-deprived person may try to "catch up" over the next few days or nights. He or she will probably experience longer than normal deep-sleep cycles as the brain readjusts.

Cycle While You Sleep

Shortly after we fall asleep, our bodies reach a very relaxed state called deep sleep. Our heartbeats, breathing rates, and digestive systems slow down. Most of our muscles become loose and floppy. An hour or so later, our muscles begin twitching. Breathing becomes faster and more shallow, and our eyes flutter underneath our closed eyelids. We enter REM (rapid eye movement) sleep. After about twenty minutes, the body relaxes again into deep sleep.

These changes from deep to REM sleep occur in roughly ninety-minute cycles throughout the night. Our deep-sleep stages gradually become lighter and shorter with each cycle until eventually we wake up.

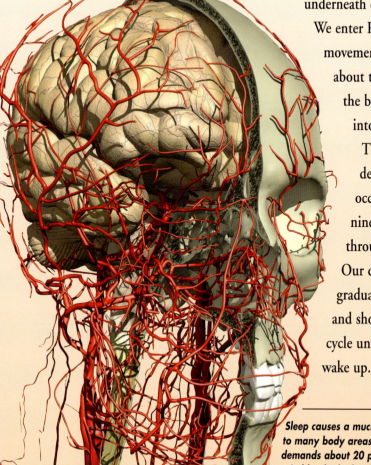

⊙ **HEALTH WATCH**

Lack of sleep can harm the body faster than lack of food. A person who cannot sleep becomes tired, confused, and forgetful and may suffer from dizziness or headaches. He or she may imagine sounds or scenes, jumble words when talking, and feel out of touch with the real world.

Sleep causes a much-reduced blood flow to many body areas, but not the brain. It demands about 20 percent of the oxygen in blood whether it is asleep or awake.

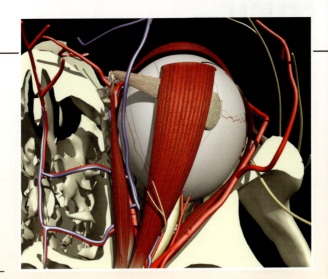

Several sets of muscles become active during REM sleep. Limbs twitch, lips quiver, and the six straplike muscles behind each eyeball produce rapid eye movements during dreams.

Most yawns last six seconds. What makes us yawn? No one knows for sure, but adults, children, and animals do it, and researchers proved that even an eleven-week-old fetus can yawn inside its mother. Many athletes also yawn before competing.

Our imaginations run wild in dreams. Most of us dream several times each night during REM sleep. We seldom remember a dream unless we wake up during the dream or just after it occurs. This painting shows Charles Dickens, the author of A Christmas Carol, experiencing a vivid dream.

Only one side of a dolphin's brain sleeps at a time. The other side stays alert, receiving information from the eyes and other senses. If danger approaches, the dolphin reacts instantly because it doesn't need to wake up.

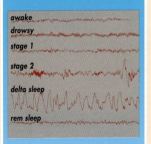

awake
drowsy
stage 1
stage 2
delta sleep
rem sleep

SLEEP PATTERNS

A recording of the brain's electrical activity in a sleeping person reveals that the brain never really shuts down. We relax completely and sleep very deeply at first but drift in and out of the various sleep stages several times as the night progresses.

It Keeps on Working

Deep inside your head, the pineal gland, part of the brain area called the thalamus, runs your biological clock and coordinates your sleep/wake cycles. The nearby hypothalamus, a tiny mass of gray matter—the "brain" of your brain—hangs below the thalamus and regulates basic body functions, such as blood pressure and body temperature. Experts cannot pinpoint the exact brain area responsible for alerting us to dangers as we sleep.

 ## TRY IT YOURSELF

Some nights we just cannot sleep. This is not a problem if it only happens once in a while. Try to help yourself fall back asleep by making sure you are not too hot or too cold. Open a window for fresh air. Imagine a peaceful, relaxing scene, such as a vacation in the warm Sun, with the waves gently lapping the shore. Swish, swish . . . zzzzzz.

An eyeball forms an almost perfectly round one-inch sphere.

Nearsightedness, or myopia, occurs when the eyeball is slightly longer than normal from front to back. The person sees only close-up objects.

Farsightedness, or hyperopia, occurs when the eyeball is slightly shorter than normal. The person needs glasses to read.

HEALTH WATCH

Eyesight is precious. Safety glasses, goggles, and similar devices shield eyes against injury and flying particles. Tinted lenses provide protection from harmful ultraviolet (solar) radiation, cut glare from sand or snow, and block intense wavelengths of light, such as from welding torches. Visit an optometrist to test your distant and near vision and all-around eye health. An ophthalmologist is an eye doctor who can also do eye surgery.

SENSES *EYES AND SIGHT*

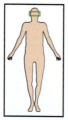

More than half of the knowledge and memories in your brain came in through your eyes as written words, images, diagrams, and scenes. Each eye detects patterns of light rays and their brightness, color, and movement and changes them into nerve signals for your brain.

Detecting Light Rays

The white of the eye (the sclera) wraps around each eyeball. At the front, a ring of colored muscle, called the iris, controls the size of the "window to the world," or pupil. Light enters the pupil, travels through the clear eye "jelly," and hits the lining, or retina, of the eye. Think of the retina as a living movie screen. It contains more than 120 million microscopic cells called rods and cones that send nerve signals to the brain when light hits them. Rods work even in dim light but do not see color. Cones see color and detail but work best in bright light.

Eye color— blue, green, gray, brown, or hazel—depends on the amount of melanin pigment within the iris. Light-sensitive blue eyes contain the least melanin.

AROUND THE EYE

A lachrymal (tear) gland arches over the top and outer corner of each eyeball. Tears flow down across the eyeball toward the nose. Six tiny muscles surrounding the eyeball swivel it in its socket, or orbit. Fat pads cushion the orbit for smooth movement.

Eyelids protect the eye from too much light by automatically squinting. They instantly shut if something comes too close to the eye. As you blink, tears containing germ-fighting chemicals cleanse your eyes and prevent them from drying out.

All animals produce tears, but only humans cry when unhappy or hurt. Emotional tears contain different chemicals than tears that flush the eyeballs with each blink. No one knows why we produce emotional tears, but a good cry releases pent-up feelings and often lessens inner tensions, which brings feelings of calmness.

Bony sockets ("orbits") in the skull protect each eyeball. The optic nerves—forward outgrowth of brain tissue—connect eyeballs to brain.

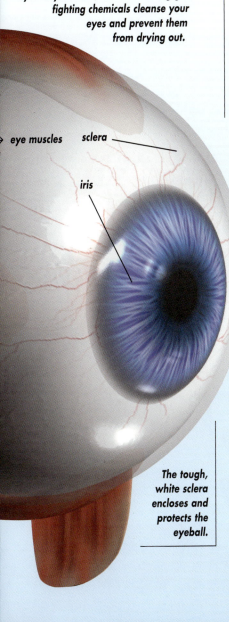

eye muscles   sclera

iris

The tough, white sclera encloses and protects the eyeball.

Near and Far

How do we judge distance? Six small, straplike eye muscles move the eyeball up, down, and side to side. Stretch sensors in these muscles signal the brain regarding the angle of the eyeball's position. When both eyes look at a nearby object, they point slightly inward. Sensors detect this closeness by the amount of inward muscle angle—the tighter the angle, the closer the object. The ciliary muscles adjust lens thickness. A thick lens focuses on nearer items; a thinner shape resolves far-away objects. We also compare sizes and judge distances by noticing how colors and details fade according to our position.

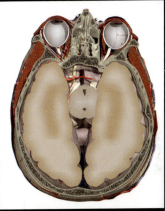

A cutaway across the middle of the head shows the short, stalklike optic nerve connecting each eye to the brain. The optic nerve is by far the most complex sensory nerve. It contains more than one million message-carrying fibers.

Light rays stimulate different combinations of cone cells to produce the more than seventeen thousand colors you might see. Three different kinds of cone cells in your retina respond to red, blue, and green hues. People missing one or more of these cone groups often lack the ability to distinguish between red and green. They are "color-blind" and only see black, white, and shades of gray.

 TRY IT YOURSELF

Visual cues help the brain interpret what it sees. Some images trick the mind. Which of the two vertical lines at right appears longer? Your eyes probably tell your brain that the right one looks longer, but the lines are equal in length.

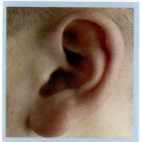
Humans can detect low and high frequencies, or pitches, of 25 to 20,000 vibrations per second. Dogs can detect much lower and higher pitches than we do.

A decibel (db) measures sound volume. Prolonged exposure to 90 db or higher, such as loud music or lawn mower noises, can permanently damage our hearing.

Gases, liquids, and solids, including the skull, all conduct sound. The ears change sound into nerve signals so that the brain's auditory cortex can analyze and make sense of them.

HEALTH WATCH

Ears are tough on the outside but very delicate inside. Germs may enter the ear canal and collect in sticky ear mucus. Mucus buildup, infection, or disease may prevent the eardrum or ear bones from moving freely—which causes pain. See a doctor if any problems develop with your ears or hearing.

SENSES *EARS AND HEARING*

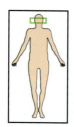

Your amazing mind constantly tunes out sounds. As you concentrate on reading, your ears hear noises around you. Yet your brain selectively ignores them—unless you hear your name or a sudden loud or strange sound.

Funnels and Drums

Our external ears act like funnels to catch sound waves. They travel down the ear tube, or canal, and vibrate a thin flap of skin—the eardrum—at the junction to the middle ear. A chain of three tiny bones called the malleus (hammer), incus (anvil), and stapes (stirrup) lead from the eardrum. These bones got their names long ago, when horses and blacksmiths were common.

Can You Hear Me Now?

As sound vibrations finally reach the inner ear deep inside the skull, they change into pressure waves within the fluid of the snail-shaped cochlea. Two tubes of fluid surround the organ of Corti that runs through the middle of

In someone with normal hearing, the stereocilia, the upper portion of the hair cells of the organ of Corti, form three rows in a "v" pattern. The amount the hairs bend depends on the sound heard.

The ear canal's hairy lining secretes a sticky wax that traps tiny pieces of dust and dirt. As we speak and eat, jaw movements loosen old wax and push it outward—cleaning the ear canals naturally.

TRY IT YOURSELF

Our two ears not only hear sounds, but also sense the direction from which they come. Sound waves seem only slightly louder to your nearer ear and reach it about $1/1{,}300$ of a second faster than the other ear. These differences help your brain determine the sound's direction. Now listen to a noise as you tilt your head so that one of your ears is much lower than the other. How does this affect your ability to determine the source of a sound?

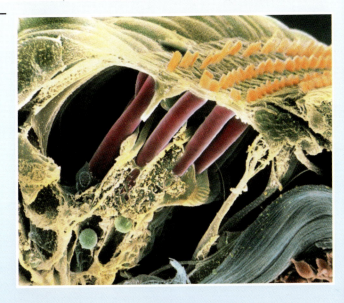

Pressure waves caused by sound frequencies cause the stereocilia (gold) that project from the hair cells (red) of the organ of Corti to bend and rub against the arch-shaped tectorial membrane, sending electrical impulses (nerve signals) to the brain.

the cochlea. Sound waves cause slight pressure waves in the fluid. The waves bend a specific section of a membrane attached to the microscopic, incredibly delicate hair cells in the organ of Corti. The swaying motion of the neatly arranged hairs fires off nerve signals to the brain's auditory center, causing the sensation we call hearing.

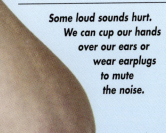

Some loud sounds hurt. We can cup our hands over our ears or wear earplugs to mute the noise.

INSIDE THE EAR

The eardrum is about the size of the nail on your little finger—but thinner than a piece of paper. It connects via the ear bones (ossicles) to the curly cochlea, which measures only 0.2 inches by 0.35 inches.

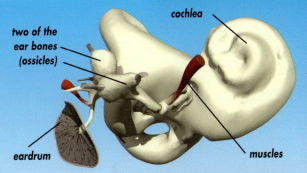

two of the ear bones (ossicles)

cochlea

eardrum

muscles

The gravity sensors in the inner ear can detect a change in position of less than one degree, or 1/360 of a circle.

The vestibular nerve carries balance information to the brain. It contains about 19,000 nerve fibers.

More than one million stretch sensors in our muscles, joints, skin, and other areas constantly monitor body position.

HEALTH WATCH

Whirling roller-coaster rides are fun. The wild movements confuse the balance sensors of our inner ears by causing the liquid and crystals within them to slosh around. Staying still for a short time afterward helps the dizziness, or vertigo, fade. Menière's disease causes constant sensations of dizziness, spinning, or falling, even when the person stands still.

SENSES BALANCING ACT

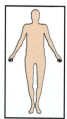

Balance is almost like a sixth sense, but it is not a sense in its own right. Instead, balance is a constant process that involves many muscles and various senses—even your eyes help you stay upright!

Balance and the Ear

Every second, the brain receives millions of signals from all over the body, which it uses for the process of balance and staying upright. Liquid-filled sacs, called the saccule and utricle, located in the inner ear next to the cochlea, contain tiny crystals. Gravity and swinging head movements cause shifts in the positions of these crystals. As the crystals move, they pull on nerves that send signals to the brain regarding the head's position and motion.

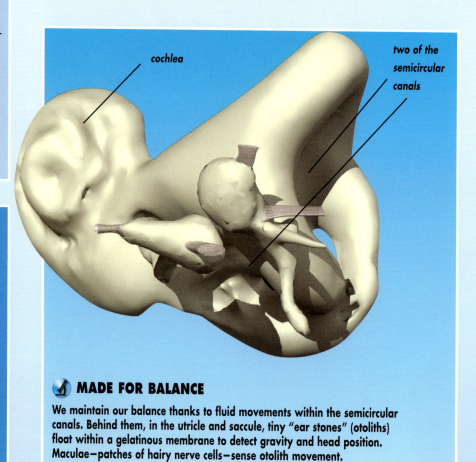

cochlea

two of the semicircular canals

MADE FOR BALANCE

We maintain our balance thanks to fluid movements within the semicircular canals. Behind them, in the utricle and saccule, tiny "ear stones" (otoliths) float within a gelatinous membrane to detect gravity and head position. Maculae—patches of hairy nerve cells—sense otolith movement.

Swirling Around

Each inner ear contains a set of three C-shaped, fluid-filled tubes called semicircular canals. As head movements cause the liquid in the tubes to swirl around, a tiny crystal pulls on nerve endings near the end of each tube. Joints and muscles located throughout the body also contain microsensors that inform the brain of their positions and amount of flexation (bending). This is how you know where your arms, fingers, legs, and feet are. Also, pressure sensors in the skin of your feet help you balance when you lean.

Just as we can learn to read or write, we can learn to balance better. Tiny stretch sensors in muscles and joints allow us to feel the position and posture of body parts. This is called our proprioceptive sense.

Cats don't really have nine lives; they simply possess better balance and react four times faster than humans. Cats also twist and arch their backs while falling and ready their legs for the shock of landing. People such as stunt workers also learn how to fall and land properly.

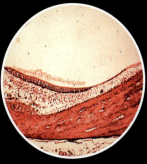

A macula, found in the saccule and utricle, is a patch of hairy nerve cells embedded in a jellylike membrane with an overlying crystal layer.

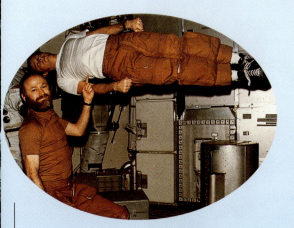

Zero gravity and lack of direction in space cause space sickness in about two-thirds of all astronauts. The lack of gravity's pull on the balance sensors gives no clues to body position.

TRY IT YOURSELF

Eyes play an important role in balance. Keep your eyes open and stand on one leg. Now close your eyes and try it. Switch feet and shift your weight. Without sight, you may begin to wobble. Open your eyes again so you don't fall over.

Gravity sensors: As the head moves, gravity pulls the macular membrane in different directions. Otoliths within the crystal layer brush against the stereocilia (blue), sending nerve signals to the brain. Another names for otoliths is ear stones.

SENSES Nose and Smell

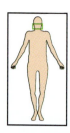

What can you smell? Your brain may already be used to the smells nearest you at this moment. The ability to ignore a scent is one of many extraordinary features of the sense of smell.

Most humans can distinguish about ten thousand smells, scents, and odors.

One of the most powerful smells comes from chemicals called mercaptans. These are present in skunk spray, and we can detect them in extremely tiny amounts of one part in twenty-five billion!

Some smell nerve signals travel to brain areas that deal with memories or emotions. Certain smells spark intense memories that seem to take us back in time and place.

Smell Patches

The nose's two holes, or nostrils, lead into twin air spaces called the nasal chambers. At the top of each chamber, an area of specialized lining about the size of a thumbnail contains a "smell patch" called the the olfactory epithelium. This patch holds an astonishing twenty-five million tall, thin smell cells packed together like the pile of a tiny carpet. Ten small hairs (cilia) stick down from each smell cell into the air space of the nasal chamber below.

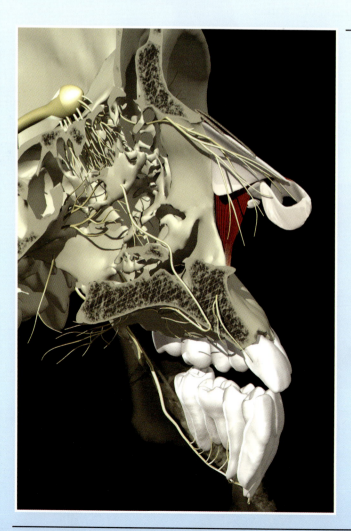

A good sniff causes air to swirl around the upper nasal chambers, which allows us to detect more smell particles. The olfactory bulb (yellow blob) just above the smell patch extends to become the olfactory nerve that leads to the brain.

Sticky Landings

Smells are actually tiny particles that drift through the air and land on the cilia in our nasal patches whenever we breathe in. Some of these particles fit into "landing sites" on the cilia, in the way that puzzle pieces fit together. When a smell particle hits the correct spot on a cilium's landing site, that smell cell sends a nerve signal to the brain.

The nasal chambers inside the nose consist of tall air spaces with shelflike ridges of bone (conchae) sticking in from the sides. Each chamber contains a smell patch in its "ceiling."

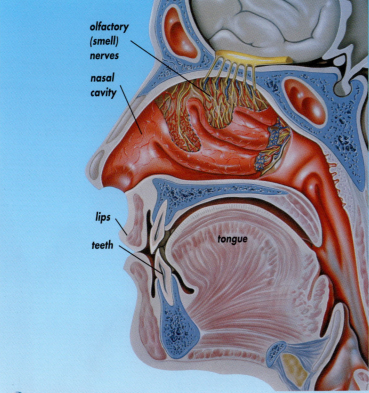

olfactory
(smell)
nerves

nasal
cavity

lips

teeth

tongue

🔧 INSIDE THE NOSE

Smell patches are located in the upper part of each nasal chamber. Tiny nerve branches gather signals from them and join to the olfactory bulb above. This setup "pre-sorts" nerve signals before they pass into the brain.

IN FOCUS
Smell Patches and Hairs

Most people do not think about "training" their noses. They get used to certain smells that they encounter every day. People who earn their living detecting scents and odors train their noses to notice or concentrate on specific smells.

Our sense of smell is fairly poor compared to many animals. Humans have about 50 million smell cells. A dog has 500 million—and its sense of smell is probably 1,000 times better than our own.

Horrible smells warn us of decay, danger, and germs. Smells alert us to food gone bad, warn of the danger of fire, or signal infection.

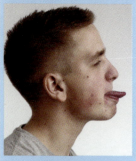

Most young people have about ten thousand taste buds.

We don't taste things as well as we grow older. By middle age, our number of taste buds falls to about eight thousand, and by old age, only about five thousand taste buds are still active.

Some people have fewer than one thousand taste buds, while others possess more than twenty thousand.

SENSES *Tongue and Taste*

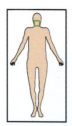

Your tongue is very useful, and not only for tasting food and drink. It moistens your lips and changes shape and position as you speak. It moves food around your mouth as you chew and dislodges food from your teeth. It helps you whistle. It can even stick out from your mouth in a display of rudeness.

Pimples and Buds

The tongue is made up almost entirely of muscle. A thin covering with small "pimples" called papillae protects the tongue. The papillae become larger and lumpier across the back of the tongue. Microscopic sensors (taste buds) on and around each papillae specialize in detecting different types of taste. Many thousands of taste buds line the front, sides, and rear of the tongue, but its central area contains very few taste buds.

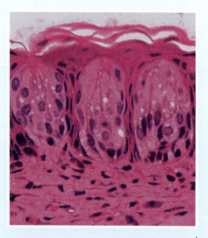

Taste buds are positioned mainly on the sides of the papillae and around their bases, not on the tongue's flat surface.

HEALTH WATCH

Ouch! It hurts when you bite your tongue or lip. This usually happens because you are thinking about something else rather than eating—or maybe you are talking and eating at the same time. Such damaged areas usually heal in a day or two. Sometimes they turn into raw, red areas called ulcers that hurt and sting when you eat. A doctor or pharmacist can advise you on treatment.

TONGUE

bitter

sour   sour

salty   salty

sweet

TASTE ZONES

We taste different flavors on specific areas of the tongue. Taste buds at the tongue's tip taste sweets. Taste buds for salty and sour foods line the sides of the tongue. Taste buds for bitterness are at the back of the tongue.

IN FOCUS
Taste Buds

The sight and smell of food can make our mouths water. Saliva (spit) moistens food, making it easier to chew. It also enhances our sense of taste by releasing flavor particles from food. Flavors must be in liquid form for us to taste them.

Flavors Galore

Ciliated (hairy) taste cells cover each taste bud. The cilia allow taste cells to detect the different chemicals in our food and drinks that produce flavor. As flavor chemicals fit into a specific "landing site" on the cilia, they cause those taste cells to send nerve signals to the brain. Our sense of taste depends heavily on our sense of smell. We can distinguish a huge number of flavors because the nerve messages from our taste buds combine with the nerve messages from our smell sensations. That is why, if you have a cold and can't smell your food, you might say the food has no taste.

A chameleon's tongue is almost as long as its whole body. If your tongue was that long in proportion to your body, you could flick it out to grab food that was too far away for your hands to reach!

Animals trust their instincts and avoid bad-tasting foods. Tongues are also useful for licking wounds, grooming, or communicating.

Like smell, taste is an early warning system that may prevent poisoning or sickness. Some sour and bitter tastes warn us of rotten, moldy, or poisonous foods that are unfit to eat.

A tongue has many jobs, including keeping the lips, teeth, and gums clean. You also need your tongue to speak clearly.

🖐 TRY IT YOURSELF

Use the dampened end of a drinking straw to put a few sugar grains on the tip of your tongue. Let them dissolve and taste the sweetness. Wash your mouth out and do the same thing, but put the grains toward the middle rear of your tongue. Can you taste anything at all?

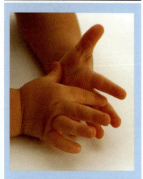

The sensitive skin of the fingertips contains fifty to one hundred microsensors in an area the size of this "o."

The same size area on the less sensitive skin on the outside of the thigh contains only one to five microsensors.

Most people tolerate a temperature difference of only a few degrees Fahrenheit (F). Water at 108°F probably feels comfortable, while water at 115°F may seem too hot and very uncomfortable.

HEALTH WATCH

Pain may be a pain, but it is also useful. It warns the brain that part of the body is about to suffer damage, or has already been injured. This allows us to avoid the harm or protect the injured part. Ignoring pain or taking too many pain pills without medical advice could cause even more damage.

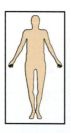

What can you feel? Unless you have just jumped out of an airplane, your body is always in contact with something. But even if you were falling through the air right now, you would feel the cool air rushing past your face and the tug of your harness when the parachute opened.

Skin Sensations

Pressure on our skin stretches and squashes microscopic touch sensors just under the surface. When this happens, the sensors fire off nerve signals along very thin nerve fibers. The fibers gather together to form thicker nerves that carry the signals from all over the body to the brain. We also feel touch if something simply brushes against our skin hairs. This occurs because nerve endings wrapped around each skin hair also send signals to the brain if the hairs sense movement. **Many Kinds of Touch Feelings** Like all of our senses, touch is more complicated than it seems. Many different sizes and shapes of microsensors

Pets feel warm and soft, two pleasing sensations of touch. Stroking them helps us relax.

No one knows why tickling makes us laugh. It works best if the tickler uses a light touch with a regular brushing motion and moves gradually across the skin. Surprise is also important—it's very difficult to tickle yourself!

IN FOCUS
Pacinian Sensors

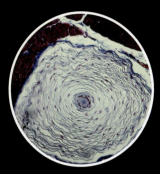

Pacinian corpuscles, sensors shaped like tiny squashed onions buried in the deep skin layers, detect pressure on your skin. Each pacinian corpuscle may be as long as 0.04 of an inch.

in the skin respond to different sensations at once, sending complex patterns of nerve signals to the brain. These patterns help us recognize what type of touch we are experiencing. The signals also give us an idea of the item's temperature, texture, and shape and whether it is moving.

Thousands of touch sensors packed together in a small space within the lips make them among our most sensitive body areas. This tight arrangement of touch cells is why babies and young children often put objects into their mouths to investigate them—and why adults enjoy kissing!

We can learn complex movements, from tying shoelaces to playing music, by touch alone. The brain concentrates on the feelings from the hands and fingers and moves the muscles in well-practiced ways.

TRY IT YOURSELF

We often identify objects simply by touch. While you cover your eyes, ask one of your friends to place about eight common items on a table. Keep your eyes closed and pick up one of the objects. You will probably guess what it is just by using your hands to understand its size, shape, weight, or texture.

SKIN SENSORS

Skin contains about six different kinds of microscopic sensors. The largest is about 0.04 of an inch across, and the smallest is one hundred times tinier.

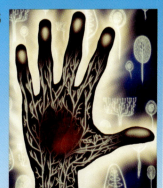

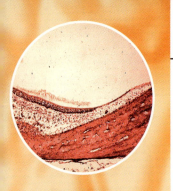

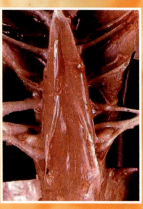

auditory related to the sense of hearing.

autonomic nervous system the portion of the central nervous system that controls automatic body processes, such as heartbeat and digesting food.

axon the long, wirelike extension from a nerve cell that transmits nerve signals to other nerve cells.

brain stem the lower, narrower area at the base of the brain that extends downward and tapers into the spinal cord. It deals mainly with automatic body processes like heartbeat.

cells the tiny building blocks of the body, which specialize into tissues and organs, such as muscles and skin.

central nervous system the brain and spinal cord.

cerebellum the lower, wrinkled area near the back of the brain that is mostly involved in muscle coordination.

cerebrospinal fluid the liquid between the meninges that helps cushion and protect the brain and spinal cord.

cerebrum the large, upper, domed area of the brain.

cilia microscopic hairlike projections found on many types of cells.

cochlea the snail-shaped structure in the inner ear that changes sound vibrations into nerve signals.

cones tapering retinal cells that work only in bright conditions and sense color.

cortex the grayish outer layer of the brain's cerebrum. It is the site of thinking, feeling, and directing muscle responses.

cranium the domed upper area of the skull that covers the brain.

dendrites short, spidery-looking branches that extend from the main body of nerve cells and receive nerve signals from other nerve cells.

dermis the inner or lower layer of skin under the epidermis. It contains blood vessels, hair roots, and touch sensors.

EEG (electroencephalogram) a paper tracing or screen display of wavy, spiky lines that represent nerve signals in the cerebral cortex.

epidermis the outermost, mostly dead surface layer of skin, which is continually being worn away.

Menière's disease an inner ear disorder marked by dizziness.

meninges three very thin tissue layers that wrap closely around the brain and spinal cord and that, together with the cerebrospinal fluid, cushion and protect the central nervous system.

mnemonic a memory aid.

motor relating to muscle movement.

nerve a cordlike tissue, specialized for carrying tiny pulses of electricity, or nerve signals, through the body.

neuron a nerve cell.

olfactory related to the sense of smell.

orbit the bony skull socket that contains the eyeball.

ossicles the ear bones: malleus (hammer), incus (anvil), and stapes (stirrup).

papillae tiny but visible lumps and "pimples" on the tongue that give it a rough surface and house the microsopic taste buds.

peripheral nervous system the system of nerves that branch from the brain and spinal cord.

proprioception the sense of knowing the position of your body in relation to where you are in space.

retina the eyeball lining that contains the sight receptors, the rods and cones.

rods tall retinal cells that sense light rays and work in dim conditions but cannot detect colors.

saccule an inner ear sac that helps detect gravity to provide a sense of balance.

semicircular canals three tiny loops in the inner ear at right angles to each other that help produce a sense of balance.

spinal cord the main nerve extending down from the base of the brain along the inside of the backbone (spinal column).

spinal nerves nerves that branch from the spinal cord between the individual bones, or vertebrae, of the spinal column.

synapses microscopic gaps between nerve fiber endings.

vertigo dizziness.

taste buds microscopic clusters of cells on the papillae of the tongue that detect sweet, salty, sour, and bitter tastes.

thalamus the "switching area" of the brain that receives sensory input and shuttles it to the appropriate area of the cerebral cortex for interpretation.

utricle an inner ear sac that helps detect gravity to provide a sense of balance.

vertebrae the twenty-six bones that make up the spinal column. The spinal cord runs down the middle of these bones.

METRIC CONVERSION TABLE

LENGTH/DISTANCE

0.04 inch = 1 mm = 0.1 centimeter
1 foot = 30.48 centimeters
15 feet = 4.57 meters

SPEED

1 mile per hour (mph) =
    1.6 kilometers per hour (kph)

WEIGHT

1 ounce = 28 grams
16 ounces = 1 pound
    = 0.45 kilograms

TEMPERATURE

Fahrenheit to Celsius
$5/9 \, (°F - 32) = °C$

I n d e x

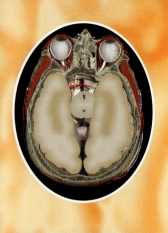

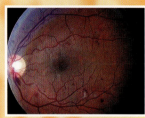

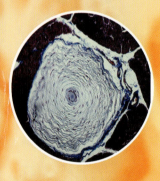

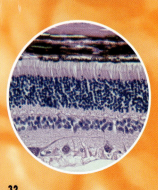

North American edition copyright © TickTock Entertainment Ltd. 2010.
First published in North America in 2010 by New Forest Press, PO Box 784, Mankato, MN 56002
www.newforestpress.com
ISBN: 978-1-84898-327-4 Library of Congress Control Number: 2010925193 Tracking number: nfp0005 Printed in the USA
We would like to thank Elizabeth Wiggans, Jenni Rainford, and Dr. Kristina Routh for their help with this book.

Picture credits: t (top), b (bottom), c (center), l (left), r (right)
Alamy: Cover (left), 5tl, 9tc, 9c, 9bc, 12tl, 13c, 14-15c, 15c, 18tl, 19tc, 19cr, 20bc, 21tc, 22-23c, 24bc, 25c, 25tr, 25cr, 26bc, 27tl, 28b. Mediscan:12–13c, 13t. Primal Pictures: Cover (right), 7tr, 9tr, 11tr, 13tr, 15tr, 17tr, 19tr, 20–21c, 21tr, 21cr, 23tr, 27tr, 29tr, 29cr. Science Photo Library: 4 (all), 9br, 11c, 13cr, 15bc, 17tc, 19c, 23cr, 26tl, 27tc, 27b, 29–30c, 29br, 30tl.